The Raccoon
and
Mrs. McGinnis

Illustrated by
Leonard Weisgard

The Raccoon
and Mrs. McGinnis

by
Patricia Miles Martin

G. P. Putnam's Sons   New York

by the same author:
BENJIE GOES INTO BUSINESS

With Love For
Amy, Bradley, Cindy, David, Debbie, Diane, Ellen,
Fritzie, Heidi, Joni, Judy, Julie, Kathy, Kinee,
Mimi, Melinda, Pauline Amey, Peter, Robinson,
Sara Beth, Shelley, Valerie and Wendy

Text ©1961 by PATRICIA MILES MARTIN
Illustrations ©1961 by LEONARD WEISGARD
Library of Congress catalog card number: 61-8028
All rights reserved
MANUFACTURED IN THE UNITED STATES OF AMERICA
Published simultaneously in the Dominion of Canada
by Longmans, Green and Company, Toronto

The Raccoon
and
Mrs. McGinnis

A little raccoon, who was almost tame,
   lived in an old apple tree.
He had a mask of black fur on his face.
He had six black stripes
   on his tail.

Near the apple tree there in the woods,
   was a little white house.
In the house lived a woman
   who was the raccoon's friend.
Her name was Mrs. McGinnis.

Once, the raccoon stopped at her window
    and looked in,
    because he was so tame.

Every night, Mrs. McGinnis put a slice
    of bread on her doorstep.
The little raccoon knew
    that the slice of bread was for him.

Mrs. McGinnis had one cow and two pigs.
Every night she tied the cow
   and the pigs under the apple tree.

One night, she stood on the step
   in front of her house.
She looked up in the sky and saw a star.
"First star I have seen tonight,"
   said Mrs. McGinnis.
   "I will make a wish."

She shut her eyes.
"I wish for a little barn,
    so my cows and pigs will be safe
    from the wind and the rain."
Then she thought of the little raccoon
    who lived in the apple tree.
"I must remember to leave a slice
    of bread for the raccoon," she said.
"He may be hungry tonight."

So she put a slice of bread
    on her step.

The raccoon looked down from his nest.
When the windows in the house were dark,
    he climbed down from the tree.

He picked up the slice of bread.
He walked into the woods
    until he came to a river.
He swished the bread in the water,
    because that is what a raccoon
    always does.
When the bread was wet, he ate it.

But the little raccoon was still hungry.
He thought he would look for
    something more to eat.
He had just started to look,
    when he saw horses
    galloping along the road.
He hid behind a tree.

Two men came galloping up.
They got off their horses
    and tied them to a tree.

"Mrs. McGinnis does not live
    far from here," the first man said.
"Let's leave our horses here,
    and go to her house.
We will not make a sound.
We will take her cow and her pigs.
She will not know they are gone
    until morning.
She will not know
    where to look for them."

The men put black masks over their faces
    and started off down the road.
The little raccoon followed.

On the men went,
    until they came to the little house
    where Mrs. McGinnis lived.
Her windows were dark.

The men did not make a sound.
Everything was still.
They took the cow and the pigs
    and started back.
The little raccoon still followed.
He was quiet, too,
    until he happened to step on a branch.
The branch broke with a big SNAP.

"What was that?" said the first man.
"It was nothing," said the other.
"Maybe some little night animal
    is playing here."

Still the raccoon followed.
Then, he happened to step on a rock.
The rock rolled down the hill
    and into the river.
It made a big SPLASH.

"What was that?" said the first man.
"It was nothing," said the other.
"Maybe little fish
    are jumping up out of the water."
The raccoon was very quiet.

Everything was still,
until he happened to bump
into a rabbit.
The rabbit jumped up
and ran down the road.

"What was that?" said the first man.
"It looked like a DEER," said the other.
"Do you know what I think it is?"
    said the first man.
"I think that someone is following us."
The little raccoon thought
    he should climb a tree,
    where he knew he would be safe.

As he was climbing,
    he looked around the tree
    to see where the men were.
In the moonlight, only the black mask
    of the little raccoon could be seen.

THE MEN WERE LOOKING
RIGHT AT HIM.

"LOOK," the first man said.
"It is ANOTHER masked bandit!"
"Don't shoot!" said the other.
"We will give you our cow and our pigs."

"We will give you our money, too,"
    said the first man.

As he ran to his horse,
    he dropped a fat moneybag
    on the ground.
It fell under the tree.

The men galloped off,
    as fast as the horses could gallop.
They did not look back.

The raccoon climbed down
and looked at the moneybag.
He took it down to the river
and swished it in the water.

The cow and the pigs
started back down the road
where Mrs. McGinnis lived.
The little raccoon followed
with the moneybag.

Because he always looked
    on the step for bread,
    he went there to look.
Then he remembered
    that he had found
    a slice of bread
    this night.
So he dropped the moneybag
    there on the step.
It fell with a big BANG.
Then he went up the tree to his bed.

Mrs. McGinnis came to the door.
"What was that bang?" she said.
She looked around.
"What is THIS?" she said.
"It is a MONEY bag.
My wish has come true.
NOW I can have a little barn
   for my cow and my pigs."

Some men came
    and soon there was a barn
    where no barn had been before.
They painted it from top to bottom.
It was a very fine barn.

At night, Mrs. McGinnis
   would look up at the sky and say:
"My cow and my pigs are safe,
   and ALL because
   I wished upon a star."
That is what she really thought!

Then she would always
   put something on her step
   before she went to bed.

When it was dark,
   the little raccoon,
   who was almost tame,
   would climb down the tree.
Then he would go to look on the step—
because he knew something....

He knew that someone
   had put a slice of bread there—
   just for him.

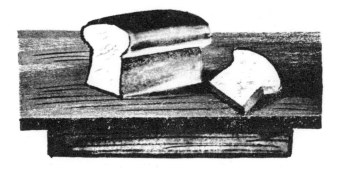

New Words in This Book

almost	raccoon
around	remember-ed
bandit	rock
bread	shoot
broke	slice
eyes	star
fur	step
hid	stripes
mask-ed	tame
moonlight	tonight
only	true

us